My First Words
A - Z
English to Indonesian

Bilingual Learning Made Fun and
Easy with Words and Pictures

by Sharon Purtill

Books

Buku

Kata-kata Pertamaku
Inggris ke Indonesia

My First Words
A - Z
English to Indonesian

Bilingual Learning Made Fun and
Easy with Words and Pictures

by Sharon Purtill

Published by Dunhill Clare Publishing - Ontario, Canada
Copyright 2021 Dunhill Clare Publishing
dunhillclare@gmail.com

Paperback edition ISBN: 978-1-990469-02-2
Digital edition   ISBN: 978-1-990469-03-9

Library and Archives Canada Cataloguing in Publications

Apple

Apel

Books

Buku

Cat

Kucing

Dog

Anjing

Elephant

Gajah

Flower

Bunga

Giraffe

Jerapah

Hat

Topi

Ice Cream

Es krim

Jacket

Jaket

Keys

Kunci-Kunci

Leaf

Daun

Milk

Susu

Nest

Sarang

Orange

Jeruk

Pail (Bucket)

Timba (Ember)

Quilt

Selimut

Rabbit

Kelinci

Shoe

Sepatu

Table

Meja

Umbrella

Payung

Vacuum Cleaner

Penyedot debu

Watermelon

Semangka

Xylophone

Gambang

Yellow

Kuning

Zebra

Zebra

Bonus Words

English and Indonesian

Let's learn common words for items
found in and around the home.

oh what
FUN

Found in the Kitchen
Yang dapat ditemukan di dapur

plate   piring

fork   garpu

spoon   sendok

knife   pisau

bowl   mangkuk

cup   cangkir

Found in the Bathroom
Yang dapat ditemukan di kamar mandi

toothpaste  pastagigi

toothbrush  sikatgigi

brush  sikat

comb  sisir

towel  handuk

Found in the Bedroom
Yang dapat di temukan di kamar tidur

bed   kasur

blankets   selimut-selimut

pillow   bantal

dresser   meja rias

toys   mainan-mainan

Found in the Living Room
Yang dapat ditemukan
di ruang keluarga

television   televisi

chair   kursi

carpet   karpet

lamp   lampu

sofa   sofa

Found Outside
Yang dapat ditemukan di luar

tree   pohon

car   mobil

truck   truk

bike   sepeda

grass   rumput

Made in the USA
Monee, IL
18 May 2022

96628384R00021